‿⤳✺⤲‿

"The Sun Between the Trees"
A Poetic Beginning
By Laurie Hraha

‿⤳✺⤲‿

ISBN: 978-1-935986-34-8

LIBERTY

UNIVERSITY.

Press

Lynchburg, VA

www.liberty.edu/LibertyUniversityPress

"I did not know Words,
Until I knew Jesus.
I did not know my place,
Until I knew Words."

- Laurie Hraha

"A Child's Story"

There is a child's story,
that I love to read,
It began at 23.
When I first met —
the real Jesus in me.

This story was simple,
Raised the child in me.
No more shame,
No more guilt,
just Jesus in me.

The regret was taken,
the weight finally lost,
it was all nailed —
to that beautiful Cross.

So when you ask,
"What's your story?"
This, will be my response —
"Look to the Cross."

"An Everyday Super Hero"

All Hallows Eve,
the night for a feast—
Filled with glossy costumes
and paper bags longing for treats.

Such fun to be had when the doorbell rings,
a father with his Super Man son—
"Trick or Treat!" the boy loudly sings.
Smiles while receiving wrapped goodies.

As they walk away—
A Thought! Sure Thunder.
Develops in my mind,
accepting the wonder.

There is no need for the stealth of night,
nor masks framed with secret
for alternative disguise—
to give us aid in Courageous Right!

We can be Everyday Super Heroes!
So long as we Choose—

This animal needs a home,
This child needs caring,
That park needs picked up,
The sick, weak, lost, and the dying.

A husband needs respect,
A wife needs love and understanding,
The children need time for family living,
All hearts deserve precious mending.

Commissioned, we are
to be just like Jesus.
His power is service.
His love, just amazing!

We can be Super Heroes,
so long as we Choose
the Highway of Jesus,
bringing others Good News!

"Bricks"

The images paved in,
a soiled-baked wound to all.
Sand mixed with flames — eye-full lust,
Built resentment and martyred white trust.

Screen, Mirage, Photograph,
Magazine and Model —
Player, Performer, Mansion Bare
Wear glamour is long offer.

Beware the Goddess in violet red
Planting what she will plunder —
a Beast of Devour will reap its Hour!
She-Vast-Waters quenched by a Baa-ing Thunder.

With this knowledge, he Chose fair warning.
Sitting crisscross in the square
his back to laid bricks —
his forehead — no longer bare.

With this knowledge, she Chose fair warning.
Sitting crisscross in the square
her back to laid bricks —
her forehead — no longer bare.

"Chores — Yes, All Life Through"

Laundry? It's never-ending.
Dishes? Not hard to find.
Vacuuming and Dusting? Will happen —
Yes, most of the time.

All the Life Cleaning —
After me, After you.

The lawn? It'll need mowing.
The cabinets? A new screw.
And, don't forget fresh light bulbs,
You'll need them soon.

All of these fixes —
Calling for me, Calling for you.

But do not be discouraged,
these chores — are actually good.
Good for me, Good for you.

Disciplines worth owning,
Disciplines worth growing,
Disciplines worth sharing —
in this Life — of Me and You.

"Come. See."

Come See the fights of old.
Conflict shed on this land.
Where blood and bodies laid to rest,
to accomplish someone's end.

You can see the trenches still,
hidden among the trees.
Where were found the bullet shells,
flanking stained canteens.

You see the dead,
they left them there
for fear and chaos
were the sound.

Of men,
Yes men,
on both sides
gathered all around.

Now years past,
one can see
the heirlooms of this war—

Rusted forks and pocket knives
surrounded by glass wall.
Picture frames and tattered vests
sobering evidence aligned.

Letters from loved ones,
Quotes of grief,
Cemented—for all time.

Come see the battlefields.
History, well told
of soldiers, men—their families,
to us, forever still war-torn.

Come see the battle's graveyards,
the dead who rest in peace.
Do not empathize this boundary—
in which they now subsist.

For only the dead, who Believe
are truly Living—
from Cross to Curtain's end
*of all **our** suffering wars.*

"Continues"

Growth in the cool spring,
Full being in the heat of summer,
Crisp changing in the fiery fall,
dead, but living in the winter.

Resting give, before nourished growth,
Hope for always, season's cleansing,
rooted soil Continues—
for all Earth.

"In but not of"

Confusion dismayed,
the course that I taught.
When called intolerant
was The Way I sought.

I don't understand.
I was but true.
But was not of
acceptable cultural mood.

What did I miss?
Which left such a mess?
You said be in the world,
but not of—is how to persist.

Reinforced! —Understand the in,
but do not become the of.
Rejected or Effective you'll be,
when sharing God's love.

"Eyes"

Oh eyes, how you hurt me.
Oh indeed, how you do.
Aware, when you are not true
to the me—that's tied to you.

Why do you wander?
Why do you roam?
At all that is beautiful,
which enters the room.

They are not your beloved,
your precious I do.
Stop drifting eyes!
Stop the pain that you do!

How can I turn you,
from that shifted gaze?
Please eyes, choose to stay
in a most honorable cage.

This you must own,
despite my loving confrontation.
A discipline only you can choose,
a transformation only self will infuse.

It will be your decision
to live as such.
As for me—
I can only hope this much.

Oh eyes! I must forgive you.
Rid the pain from my heart.
To forgive and forget,
your dark rovering part.

Oh Lord! Please help me!
I need to forgive,
the one, You entrusted.
Oh how shall I forgive?

The anger is growing.
I'm depressed in my skin.
I must choose love, I promised—
But how? I'm empty within.

How did You do it?
To all who betrayed You.
You took Your cup.
Yes, You drank it in full.

Lord, let me swallow too.
It's dark in the garden—
As You forgave me,
I forgive too.

"Freedom Spirit"

Freedom Spirit, Freedom Spirit!
Why can't they see?
I died and gifted
the All Living Me.

Freedom Spirit, Freedom Spirit!
Oh, certain and true,
that to ignore You—
turns a back to Precious Fruit.

Freedom Spirit, Freedom Spirit!
If only they Soared!
Yet, choose to clip wings,
and force open locked doors.

Freedom Spirit, Freedom Spirit!
Oh why should We be—
Expected inside rubrics
or perfectionist pleas?

Freedom Spirit, Freedom Spirit!
If only once more—
I meant Loving Instruction,
not critical bore.

"God Knew"

God knew what He was doing,
when He created me.

This truth was not so easy,
in the world labeled what "to be."

I doubted and disliked,
how You had knitted me.

It mocked in expectation
of the life that I would see.

Although the effort of "to be,"
All I thought created wonderful me —

I was better off.
I was better off.

As "to be" — Your created Lamb,
crafted most lovingly.

God knew what He was doing,
when He created me.

"God's Galloping Grace"

Have you ever watched
God's Galloping Grace?

It's strong beauty charging,
the most greenest of place.

It's hair blowing,
to the lift of its pace.

With eyes filled with Fire,
Lit—for the scope of God's face.

"God's Children"

Children are the art of God's handiwork.
Their colors are Pure and Bright,
but the world looks to paint dark shadows
over these Beautiful Souls of Delight.

Thankfully,
God gave us a tool
to chip off the stained gloom
to let the Light of the Vivid—Blaze forth Anew!

Thank you Jesus,
Precious Jesus,
in giving us All—
the way to remain, Children of God.

"Christmas is Coming, what should I Give?"

Folding the laundry,
trees bare outside,
the phone starts its ringing
my husband says, "Hi."

"Christmas is coming,
what should I give?
The Black Out is Friday,
the sales will be Big!"

I thought calm and quiet—
of the extent he could measure.
So much temporary toys—
pure Joy comes not in plastic pleasure.

I twiddled the cord,
and revealed the extension,
"Give the First Gift,
of the very First Christmas."

The receiver was silent,
I hoped not offend.
Maybe, just maybe
Thoughts were on a New bend.

Days began to dwindle,
snow thinly dust,
as my husband plans
a merry Christmas.

He gives me a wink,
I respond with a smile.
The children are cheering,
"It's the Eve of the Child!"

It started with carols,
O' Holy Night!
And ended with Lanterns,
<u>filled</u> with the Light.

The Story was read,
children listening arm-tight.
Then next was the Nativity,
set-up just Bethlehem right.

But in the tiny manger,
that was left empty.
As we told our children,
"Wait till Christmas morning."

Christmas Day they arose,
hurried wonder down the stairs.
Direct eyes in the Manger,
the Baby now swaddled there.

"He's here! In our house!"
The cry, oh so heart tender
as singing with the angels,
"Emmanuel, God with Us!"

My husband acknowledged,
"It is Baby Jesus.
The very First Gift,
of the very First Christmas."

I'll never forget—
that Christmas we shared,
Now it's our grandchildren's.
The Christmas Gift <u>hoped</u> for All Years.

"Law and Passion"

Aristotle termed wisely so,
that "the Law is reason,
free from Passion."
As most bar students know.

And it is this quote,
that protects judicial stone
amidst the demeanors
and those sent death row.

Having this hearing—
supremely logic in treatment.
Governments and courts upholding,
innocent till proven guilty.

Amendment is fair,
Justice's conduct will apply.
But where does that leave Passion?
God's Son on a cross to die.

Horrifying this treatment.
Appearing an act without reason—
Innocent Passion, Condemned for the Law,
God's atoning sacrifice for all.

Though Law still applies—
this one relief is true,
Forgiveness is Free Passion
Paid in Full—if you Choose.

"In Heaven I'll Swim with Dolphins"

In Heaven—

I'll swim with Dolphins.
I'll even hug a Bear.
I'll run wild with the Mustangs.
And, walk the meadow with a Deer.

The one thing I wonder…
that I'll have to wait and see,
is if I will fly with the Eagle—
through sky and wind…

Oh, Eternity—

"Meditation"

The nails did not keep You there.
The nails did not keep You there.

You had the Power to get down.
You had the Power to get down.

You chose to Stay there.
You chose to Stay there.

Because, You thought of me—
Because, You thought of me—

a Love worth dying for.
a Love worth dying for.

"Meditation, Tomorrow"

How many people,
have made me feel
that I—am not
worth loving?

How many people,
have I made feel
they—are not
worth loving?

How awful,
this truth.
But, You—
brought a new truth.

We are all worth loving.

How many times,
have made me feel
that I—am not
worth loving?

How many times,
have made others feel
they—are not
worth loving?

How awful,
this truth.
But, You—
brought a new truth.

We have been, are, and will be—loved—at all times.

"Tis' the 7th Day"

Get up my love!
Tis' the 7th day!
The time to venture and play,
for work is done
and there is some sun—
to start this new, glorious day!

"Naptime for my Kitty"

It's playtime for my Kitty—
So, grab her favorite toy mouse.
And maybe with some catnip—
place it tactfully for her to pounce.

And, then there's her laser—
a mad chase for her to capture.
Sometimes I feel guilty,
there's no reward for her effort.

So instead I give her treats,
fortified with tasty liver.
A feline's favorite snack,
crunched and swallowed with great vigor.

Then she slouches up to bed,
tired from all the adventure.
She gently massages the fleece just right,
and curls into a fluff ball figure.

It's naptime for my Kitty—
So, draw the curtains tight.
For daytime is her rest time,
and darkness is her light.

"No More Time"

As I sat, as he preached,
of a place without Time —
I could only agree,
what a Good Rest it will be.

"Help Me Please"

Can someone help me please?
This line is hard to tread.
The rope is constantly moving,
and fear has me stuck at its head.

Can someone please help me?
Since I am at a loss,
for to walk this thread —
Perfection — is to get me safely across?

This expectation shifts relentlessly,
with the changing fads.
Creates such an anxst in me,
one misstep could be bad.

To be a constant acceptance,
in spite my real, redeeming self?
Instead, I cut Trap's death tightrope,
Turn from its approval — and value Truth! above all else.

"What are you Applauding?"

What are you applauding,
when you rustle like so?
Is it dancing?
Or waving?
When the sky screams,
"CRE—SCEN—DO!!!"

"Oh Vegetables"

Oh Vegetables,
colors of rainbow delight.
I don't understand—
why T-Rex and sugar fairies
frown upon you.
Then there are the times,
when you're swimming in ranch
or melting in cheeses.
Why lessen the garden's flavor?
Your fibrous form is a natural choice.
Planted grown product with
the dawning of time.
Oh Vegetables,
Created edible favor,
that lovingly add
to the health of all figures.

"Out"

When it was just me,
I wanted out.
This body, this name—
Out! Out! Out!

This prison bar cage,
stuck as myself.
To shed my skin,
and exit—out, out, out!

But could this be
an answer to me?
I'd still exist as
Me! Me! Me!

A swelled sponge,
absorbed with pain.
Desperate for wringing
Out! Out! Out!

Then came willing hands,
unplugging the drain.
Replenishing a New name,
I remain, I remain.

This will be
the answer to me.
I shall exist with
You. You. You.

When it was just me,
I wanted out.
But—it is not just me,
In You I remain. In You I stay.

"Peace"

What do you do to be at Peace?
Where do you go to find Rest?
To be still,
To be calm,
When all else seems wrong?

I knew a friend that did the dishes.
My father, he quietly prayed.
My husband works to calm his tenses —
household fixes, a handy plot.
My mom watches good fun tennis,
and enjoys cheering a lot.

But for me, as each before me
most different and unique,
I love to groom the horses
so tenderly and sweet.

I love to look them in the eye
gazing most attentively
and stand amazed by what I read
Loved by God, and now —
Loved by me.

Have you ever brushed a horses' mane,
as if it were your own?
To gently get the tangles out
and brush it smoothly down.

Or ever bought a soft-touch brush,
and massaged all the face?
Rubbing the ears so soothingly,
cleaning the nostrils out,
wiping away the eye crust —
so no flies can hang about.

This is such a peaceful treat
for the heart of me.
To see those big, round eyes
thankfully starring back at me.

The joys of our souls connect.
The hope for all to see,
The Great Plan for all Creation —
is to Love Eternally.

"Pure Beauty Arise Incorruptible"

Beauty was a precious girl,
with a heart that shined
and words that loved—
but grew without root,
the sure True fill.

Without this True fill,
when teases and taunts
became her daily pill—
ignored and rejected
was her loving skill.

Sad and confused,
longing for some friends—
she realized what was acceptable
and decided to join in.
This sure fix—for appreciation to begin.

With a shutter in the mirror,
she made her resolution
and began the manipulative plan.
She started with the teases—
Erasing all subjected contraband.

Beauty adorned—
the straightening of hair,
complexion enhanced,
and clothes flirty tight—
everything changed to popular right.

For social conditions—
Beauty enticed,
studying company glamour prescribed.
Mocked in exultation to frame her just right;
acted as such, this diva divine.

Her mind contorted and turned
being conventional lustrous sought.
Devoted to her pinnacle thrill—
continued to build,
what splendor brought.

On she lived from high school
through college—
but Beauty was suffering vacant,
addicted to the life she lived—
Conditioned and Controlled within.

Then one day—
an Invitation comes her way.
By a bulletin portrayed,
in a coffee shop of all place.
To a church service
called—Good Friday.

There she sat in the pew,
feeling a bit awkward too.
But as the service began
and the sermon approached,
Beauty was intrigued at most.

As she heard of a man
despised and rejected
just for the reason of who He is—
something was stirring
reflective thought, no longer blurring.

She saw a young girl—clear.
Without wanting escape
from a long ago pain
she falsely replaced.
Years—without embrace.

She saw the innocence of herself—
that was despised and rejected.
Teased wrongly so—
yet she allowed this dictation
to how she would grow.

Turned and wielded
to be as they sowed.
But this man—
would Not be derailed
in how He would go.

*He stood steadfast
to the truth He beholds.
His identity —
the Sure Way
for All to know.*

*As the service ended,
with the death of God's Son.
Beauty with congregation,
slowly shuffled along
Depth comprehensive —
a Silent Song.*

*To the bookstore Beauty continued,
still — quietly.
She picked up a Holy Bible,
paid the clerk, said thank you,
and drove home — heart wondering.*

*She scanned the Bible's contents,
unsure where to begin.
But inside the index —
a Word was caught!
Quite surprised was this thought.*

*The word "beauty," boldly printed
curious attention — as if He knew.
She scanned the list of verses,
offering distinct comfort
for All who pursue.*

*She read the Scriptures,
contemplating His way —
but it was verse 3 through 4 in first Peter,
chapter 3 — that opened her heart
and convinced her to stay.*

*In the midst of her decision,
identity of her long-chosen way —
tears interrupted the blush
and the powder that laid.
Repentance was fully made.*

Regretting her path
and the emptiness it gave—
while missing the girl she decided away.
Beauty, hoping for forgiveness,
and the path that He laid….

Comes an interruption
from the Love—
that conquered the grave.
"I hear your heart's cry,
and all you confessed."

"You are forgiven.
You knew not what you did.
The darkness is over.
You've seen the Great Light!
New Life Begins—on this very night!"

"I was with you,
when you read this True fill.
Genuine beauty—that will heal.
I know you turned from that path
that led you so ill."

"I see your heart's devotion,
the desire for what's real.
You will be that ornament,
a priceless Spirit, meek and mild—
an unending sight, known as My child."

The next day she spent,
spending time with her Lord.
Reading the Bible and listening—
to the Friend she adored.
Unconditional love—forevermore.

And out of this Love,
she would now grow
a true heart that shined
and loving words
that would faithfully fill.

Easter Sunday she came,
warmly greeted by family,
no silence this day—

All joined in praise!
singing He is Risen!

And, while singing Hallelujah,
Something again stirring—
reflective thought, no longer blurring.
She saw a tomb—her heart.
The one Jesus knew.

And in front of the tomb,
stood the Lord dressed in white.
Removing the stone—
with outstretched hands—calling,
"Pure Beauty Arise!"—

She knew His voice,
she volitionally followed—
He hugged her anew,
Rejoicing! —
"Incorruptible is you!"

With tears she smiled,
now a beautiful woman
who came to Good Friday
Hoping for change,
and Receiving—Years of Embrace.

"I Run the Race of Faith."

I love to run.
I've always dreamed of being
a phenomenal runner.

I've dreamed of being
a stellar athlete for God.
I would be an athlete
who'd minister to so many people.

But my dreams are not always
His dreams.

As of now, I'm grateful that I could run.
As of now, I'm grateful for my modest ability.
I enjoy the blessing of being healthy,
taking care of the one body I have.

I'm grateful for this discipline.
For as of still, I run.
I Run the Race of Faith.

Now, I dream of a Faith.
Faith instilled by God, and for God.
It's the hardest race
I've ever chosen to run.

It costs so much.
It wears you down.
It makes you question.
It makes you suffer.

It causes pain..

Sometimes, you think—
you are going to lose,
Or you feel—
You've already lost.

However—
*You **still** Run the Race of Faith.*
It's worth the Finish.
For what would Faith be,
without the challenges of running?

Please remember, it is worth the Finish.
Run the full Race, for a fulfilled Faith.

For the Race is already Won,
Won by God's Son,
He authored Faith's Course
for anyone to run!

The race that He laid,
does not depend on me.
Keep my eyes on Him,
and stride faithfully His way!

I keep moving forward with these thoughts in my head.
But, the thought that surpasses them all—
That keeps me striding ahead—
My favorite—

Is the moment I enter my last lap,
the one that leads to the Finish.

I enter the stadium of Heaven.

It's a golden realm surrounding.
The noise is overwhelming.
The angles are singing,
The saints are cheering,
They shout for joy—
"Keep running! You're nearly there!"

And, as I look to the 'nearly there'—

I SEE Him!
I finally SEE Him!
*I see Him— **the Finish Line.***

The reward I've been Waiting for,
Hoping for.
It is God's Son with open arms.

I run.
I run!
And, I run!

The singing and the cheering is so loud!
The singing and the cheering is so proud!
I run to Him, I run to Him!

And as I finally embrace
the Finish Line,
and Hug my Savior divine—

He smiles,
and sweetly speaks,
"It is Finished.
Well done, faithful one."

I cry.
I weep.
As He gently removes
the running shoes from my feet,
and lovingly speaks,
"Your Faith is Complete."

"The Authority"

I feel like a dog,
whose Master has gone away.
I just want to lie down
and forever lay.

It is Your return,
the Promise I keep.
That stirs me to be—
the Path paved in Ink.

To see Your face,
when this Wait finally ends.
You gave me a Hope—
the reason I live.

"Scout"

It was such an awful then,
To see you breathe your last.

But then I received the Rainbow's treat,
Jesus' promise to All who surpass.

Our relationship will not end—
In Heaven, we will forever play again.

It is such Good News!
I Believe! My faithful, loyal friend.

"Sculpture Raised from ruff Bay"

I was but a lump of clay.
So lost and dejected,
to death! I sorely begged—
on the cliffs of Ruff Bay.

But prod came Your finger
and a mold gave way.
Time was long—
the work You portrayed.

But by Your commitment
and Your loving plan,
You crafted me Sure armor—
safe from the steep, sunken grave.

Now, I'm Your sculpture!
Laden with precious Stone—
that the builder's rejected,
but welded a Garden of Hope.

And tis' this Hope,
that 3-D is formed.
Once cold, soft clay—
Now Reborn!

Pure water applied,
with Hands strong and firm.
Then solidifying fire,
"Stands—Me! Sculpted Resolve!"

It was long ago—
I was but a lump of clay.
So lost and dejected, but now—
Your sculpture Raised from ruff Bay!

"Thanksgiving this Year"

Gathered at my bedside,
with heavy heart I stare.
Wondering if this Thanksgiving,
will he again be lying there?

Despite this looming question,
I willingly prepare
the menu of Thanksgiving,
I hope we share this year.

Turkey's a must,
Green bean casserole,
mashed potatoes and gravy,
his favorite desert — to top of the evening.

I finally submit
to another solo night,
and commit the same prayer
I've prayed since his flight.

Newlyweds we are.
He chose to make right,
of the love that we shared
before his deployment to — out-of-sight.

It's been seven months,
only one month left —
but I won't count my chickens,
before they actually hatch.

Much grief I have heard.
Much grief we now know —
of friends laid injured,
or friends with departing sorrow.

With tears in my eyes,
I'm reminded of a verse
of a God who protects,
and has kept Safe thus far.

I repeat the same prayer,
that I already prayed—
knowing He loves me
with each I send His way.

Dear Lord,
Please protect him,
in his comings and goings.
Let no harm come to his tent.

Please Lord,
Bring him home—alive—
Whole in mind, body and spirit—
Shielded free from the Enemy's grasp.

And with an Amen,
I'm still left in thought
of the Love that I treasure,
the Love that You brought.

I stare at his picture,
holding his pillow so tight,
and wish that this Thanksgiving
he'll be home from the fight.

The weeks finally pass,
The weight finally gone,
My Love is finally—finally—
on his way home.

Thank you Lord,
for the peace! —we now gratefully receive.
I'll treasure Your gift—
and Rejoice when we meet!

What a wonderful Thanksgiving.
A Feast! —Full and Complete!
My eyes glisten, with Your candlelight—
*at my Love, You so **graciously** brought home to me.*

"The Awakening, Pure Melody"

Pure Melody, innocent and sweet
grew up...
just round the corner,
on Ever Essence Street.

She laughed and played,
like most at three.
Then came the age,
where she climbed and scraped her knee.

She was well-mannered,
a sure joy to teach.
Raised correctly,
Involved—that loving family.

Scholastic, church-going,
athletically sound.
One honored senior—
successfully bound.

Accomplished full ride,
the talk of the town.
Her parents so proud,
their Miss Valedictorian crown.

How focused, exemplar,
this young woman at 18.
Now, gifted-collegiate-potential!
Venturing on—Pure Melody!

Her appearance—attractive.
Personality—a crush.
Talented grades and good sporty fun
Ideal—for a special someone…

but Pure Melody, too tempting to see,
desirously intimidating
for intoxicated man now prowling.
Speculated age? Twenty…maybe?

Her roommate returning,
a door left unlocked,
The last sleep of innocence
Pure Melody could trust.

Now Melody, sweet Melody
Alone and so lost
retracts from her studies,
her sports, and her Cross.

Home she wanders,
for safety and rest.
Her parents—so caring,
with broken hearts—They persist.

Melody, poor Melody,
afraid and hiding.
Anger, depression, now linger
beneath the colorless lining.

Her reflection she's rejecting.
Her light turned storm-gray.
She accomplishes nothing
day after day.

Then suddenly it raptures,
bitter grief—deranged.
The darkness emerging,
but rotting it remains.

Her father, a preacher,
runs to hug her so tight.
Repeating "I love you",
Morning, Noon, and each Night.

Melody, poor Melody,
she looks in the mirror.
Cringing, despising—
as she steps nearer.

She can't stand it much longer.
She destroys what she sees.
Shattered glass—now resembles
the dead soul that proceeds.

Her parents—
they hold her,
Their poor Melody;
Wisely praying—so perpetually.

Faithful to Jesus,
the hope which they cling,
strum true chords of healing
to their daughter—now 23.

"Melody, Oh Melody,
My Dear, come near.
Your loss is My loss.
Your brokenness—My Tears.

Melody, Oh Melody,
Please come seek Me still.
Your heart needs precious mending,
freedom from filth that relentlessly fills."

Reaching for what is Dusty
Desperate for change
Melody turns on the Light
and opens the Page.

A daily read He becomes,
Understanding this Son.
Words filling up—
something New has begun.

One cloudy day,
with some mist and some doubt
Melody, pursuing Melody,
was searching about…

There was a verse
that came silently Strong.
It was God's devotion
that renewed the Sacred song.

Wash in His blood
the sin and the pain,
be Robed anew
His <u>pure</u> Adorning of <u>you</u>.

And with that she fell
on her knees to the floor,
and cried volitionally to Him,
"<u>Cleanse Me Pure Forevermore!</u>"

And that night she slept,
with no dreams to abhor—
just sweet "I love you's"
whispered gently by her Lord.

Her witness is simple,
the relationship she Trusts—
"Pureness cannot be taken.
Pureness is Word Awakened."

In Jesus Christ,
Awakened and Pure
Melody; Resurrected Melody
—Lives On!

"The Debate"

Upon the stage stood two lecterns,
neither labeled, but wood-bare.
And, on walked the debaters,
with silence, but prepared.

The setting was unusual,
not what you'd politically expect.
For the topic was about 'Hiding'—
A most unlikely discussed prospect.

First campaigned the Left—
declaring acting as a strength,
"Don't be Natural, Look Natural!"
… "Imperfections must be Covered!"

"Personal Image and Social Behavior—
Do not Foolishly Neglect!
These are necessities and delicacies
that must be Layered properly to Protect!"

On and on, Left went.
Promoting all the same—
Constantly spieling and consuming
to its relentless claim.

Then came a quiet, Sure voice—
whispering Left's name.
It was gentle, but firm, the way Right spoke
to address Left's pursuing game.

"You may choose to play Hide n' Seek
Never to be Found—
but for where your existence will be—
forever underground."

"The Staff Meeting"

Satan:
Ah, thank you for coming….Deception, Goddess, Doubt, Addiction, Confusion and Discouragement. How are my Agents of Death?

Agents:
Planting the way-side—what we will plunder!

Satan:
Wonderful! Excellent! Therefore, it is time for reports. Goddess—ladies first.

Goddess:
My images are pouring in. Men and women, their teenagers, fall every time for my tactics. Lust, sexual immorality, rape, jealousy, vanity, adultery (interrupted)

Confusion:
Well, I might have had something to do with that. I get credit for sexual confusion.

Goddess:
Oh, yes. We doubled-teamed on my last adultery case, this pathetic fool resolved not to cheat, but Confusion came in and mixed up the fool's emotions. Successfully, the fool's resolve faltered.
(Snickers of evil laughter all around)
You think—They'd put a stop to it by now, but they never learn. You think—they would know better to not allow my images and ways.

Satan:
Yes, well, let's make sure they don't think. Let's keep the advantage that most of humanity is still being subject to our ill thought. We don't want them to think like our Enemy.
(Agents nod and agree around the room)
But, excellent temptation work Goddess—thank you for your idol ways. Confusion—superb assistance. I hope the spouse was left bitter, angry, and hurt. And, the children confused and saddened.

Confusion
and Goddess:
Absolutely.

Satan:
Lovely. I love when the species of man chooses our way— such wonderful destruction! Who's next?

Addiction: *I too am helping. I have great means. Modesty, Purity, and
                  Discipline are trampled thin. Alcohol, Drugs, Internet,
                  Pornography, Work, Money—Men, women, and children
                  are dependent. Time is wasted on infatuation and
                  compulsion. Families suffer
                  (interrupted)*

Deception: *Give credit, where credit is due, Addiction. Families suffer
                  because they are deceived by my mind and emotional tricks.
                  I take their emptiness and make them feel and think of false
                  cravings. I point them to those means. You keep them in those
                  means, Addiction.*

Satan: *Wonderful! Excellent, Deception. Addiction I want to see
                  more means used by Internet and Technology. Let them
                  relate more to machines then directly with each other. Let
                  "time for each other" become non-existent. That will allow
                  other agents to perpetrate. Goddess, lovely Goddess,
                  advertise yourself when that happens. Tear them apart!
                  (Loud evil laugh)
                  (Agents nod and smile)
                  Also, Deception, help Addiction with filling their time to not
                  read the Enemy's blasphemous book!
                  (Deception eagerly nods)
                  Doubt, looming Doubt, are my subjects still skeptical of the
                  Enemy?*

Doubt: *I keep their backs facing the Enemy. I fill their minds, hearts,
                  and souls with myself. Their beings are uncertain. Their ears
                  and eyes see our work. Their thoughts are me.*

Satan: *What great relief. Thank you, Doubt. They must not find the
                  other way. They must not realize all they have to do is turn
                  and be devoted to the Enemy.*

                  Discouragement, is the remnant boarded up?

Discouragement: *With the help of all our Agents, my work is successful. They
                  are discarded in ministry. With the help of all our Agents,
                  there are too many barriers. They are weakened and
                  silenced. They are rejected by our subjects.*

Satan: *Good. Excellent work everyone. Continue the plague.
                  Meeting adjourned.*

"The Sun between the Trees"

I walked a road,
where the Sun —
Danced —
between the trees.

It seemed to follow me,
tree after tree.
Mesmerizing my eyes,
so brisk and chilly.

When I turned back,
it followed me still —
dancing between the wood —
not so lonely, this hill.

It is Your warm presence.
I concede. I concede —
the Dance does not follow me,
but Calls me — Longingly.

"Where is He going?"

Where is He going?
What is He doing?
Wandering that valley,
surveying rocky trenches?

Why the effort?
What's the longing?
For the scaling
He's projecting?

What's that you say?
A lost lamb needs a way?
So He searches all day—
for the one that wandered away?

Is this true? Is this what He does?
Leaves the sheep fold in the hills,
So the one will not fall prey,
to the wolf's pursuing game?

That's quite the shepherd.
Forsaking none—
and valuing—each one.
Yes, He values each and every one.

"Where to begin?"

Where to begin?
When the plummet,
goes! Descending—
to the sewer maze below.

Stuck in the tunnel,
nostrils burn with regret
of the mire that has followed
a choice—to consequence sick.

The surrounding is dismal,
cemented darkness and clout.
Hopeless, you wander—
thinking you'll find a way out.

Weight on your shoulders,
feet mucking about
in the world you created—
the dark whole—lead by doubt.

Blindly you walk,
hands guiding your route.
'Til finally you fall—
lost and desperate you shout!

Lonely without a rescue,
incessant hours of despair,
knees to your chest — true remorse flows —
from the maze of shadows hidden below.

Light starts to peak,
unsure effort comes half-way
of a someone you hurt
in a most horrific way.

Yet the Light that they bring
is a Light that they study,
of a Man who forgives
and restores what is muddy.

You willingly stand,
and admit released grime.
Complete the other half —
Full light begins to Shine!

And out of the maze,
You successfully climb
to walk above the tunnel
hand in hand — for all time.

"Words do not fail me."

Words do not fail me.
So, I seek Words—
Trying to lace—
Your truth to be heard.

Let me not sink,
into silent salt lake—
Light's Ambition for all—
is to STAY AWAKE!

Knock, knock! Please help me.
Please help me to converse,
the Sure footed path—
You created on this Earth.

My mind is determined.
My heart is filled up.
This being is expanding—
all, which You made capable of asserting.

You are the Words,
I desire to sow!
A tenant You left me—
Highest offering to grow.

When the Master returns,
What depth will He find?
Words do not fail me.
How You want me to Shine!

How I long to be faithful,
to the Vine of my branch.
Producing good fruit—
and nurturing Your land.

The talents You gave me,
All according to Your plan—
You love me so greatly:
Double! Triple! For the palm of Your hand!

By Laurie Hraha

9 781935 986348